Awaken & Train META LEADERSHIP

A modern catalyst for Corporate Social Responsibility

Laurent Zecchinon

Author

Laurent Zecchinon

Titre

Awaken & Train META-LEADERSHIP
A modern catalyst for Corporate Social Responsibility

ISBN : 9798872822349

Independently published

First edition

Photo: Aimy Zecchinon

DEDICATION

This book is dedicated to everyone working to make a world more ethical, more balanced, more congruent, especially in the business field.

TABLE OF CONTENTS

ACKNOWLEDGMENTS

I would like to thank all the people who have inspired me to reflect on this subject and who have contributed, directly or indirectly, to the writing of this book.

Those who led me by example, inside and outside the business world. You help me become a better person by feeling, thinking, and performing better.

Those who in contrast exemplified real mediocrity. You inspire me to find and create something much better.

I have a special thought for the people, family, and friends, who have accompanied me on this path, sometimes for decades. They will all recognize themselves (which, by the way, ensures that I don't forget anyone.

1 - INTRODUCTION

"If you want to build a ship, don't herd people together to collect wood and don't assign them tasks and work, but rather teach them to long for the endless immensity of the sea."

- *Antoine de Saint-Exupery*

During my last 25 years, I had the opportunity to work in several environments: university, small biotechs, a big pharma, a secondary school, and a hospital. Afterwards, when I became a coach/consultant/trainer (different facets of the same profession in my opinion), I also supported several other businesses i.e. the construction sector, a law firm or even a tourist office.

This variety of professional environments made me discover several structures, cultures & leadership styles. Some were inspiring and growth-oriented, others not.

When I made the decision to take full accountability of my personal life and development, I chose to explore this field looking for answers to two questions. Would I do better? How?

I firmly believe that better connecting the human potential with a more conscious and respectful humanity could or even should be achieved through business organizations and entrepreneurship.

This book is therefore intended to provide insights for those who are looking for a better workplace, where people, environment and economy are thriving together, and not one at the expense of the other.

As **Tony Robbins** says, complexity is the enemy of execution. Today, too many organizations (businesses or administrations) are really constipated, lacking both performance and wellbeing, due to an excess of internal **complexity**. Despite their willingness to change or transform regularly, using different well-known methodologies, they continuously fail to meet the double-objective of human and business fulfillment.

On top of that, a modern organization needs to be both stable and agile to thrive in our **VUCA** world (Volatile, Uncertain, Complex and Ambiguous). In brief, it means that the world is now much more interconnected (thus interdependent) and that things can evolve much faster than before, with both more challenges and opportunities.

Corporate Social Responsibility

Corporate social responsibility (**CSR**) is the responsibility borne by companies as regards the effects they have on society. They are no longer evaluated only from an economic perspective, but also from a societal and environmental one.

It can be viewed as a **continuous process of improvement**, in which companies incorporate social, environmental, and economic considerations into the overall management of the company in a voluntary, systematic, and coherent way.

CSR is based on a range of tools - **norms, standards, and labels** - which make it possible to measure the authenticity of these practices and their added value, and to maximize their effects for both the company and society.

Many companies view CSR as an integral part of their brand image, believing that customers will be more likely to do business with brands that they perceive to be more ethical. Some company founders are also motivated to engage in CSR due to their **convictions**.

Engaging in CSR means that, in the ordinary course of business, a company is operating in ways that **enhance society** and the environment instead of contributing negatively to them.

CSR initiatives are often broken down into **four categories**: environmental, philanthropic, ethical, and economic responsibility. **Environmental** initiatives focus on preservation of natural resources, while **philanthropic** initiatives focus on donating to worthy causes that may not relate to a business. **Ethical** responsibility ensures fair and honest business operations, while **economic** responsibility promotes the fiscal support of the goals above.

Environmental responsibility is deeply rooted in the stewardship of our planet. Simply put, it involves the commitment to enhance and conserve natural resources affected by the company's operations. This commitment is manifested through various initiatives such as (i) minimizing pollution, waste, natural resource consumption, and emissions throughout the manufacturing process, (ii) actively participating in the recycling of goods and materials, (iii) offsetting negative impacts by replenishing natural resources or supporting causes that mitigate the company's environmental footprint (e.g., committing to plant an equivalent or greater number of trees than those removed during deforestation), (iv) consciously distributing goods by opting for methods with minimal impact on emissions and pollution, and (v) developing product lines that align with and respect these environmental values.

In essence, environmental responsibility strives not only to minimize harm but also to contribute positively to the overall health and sustainability of our natural world.

Philanthropic responsibility revolves around the transformative impact a company can have on society through its actions and contributions. It extends beyond profit-making to address how a company utilizes its resources to enhance the well-being of the world. This encompasses (i) donating profits to charities or causes that resonate with the company's values, (ii) engaging in transactions exclusively with suppliers or vendors that share the company's philanthropic ethos, (iii) supporting employees in their philanthropic pursuits by offering time off or matching contributions, and (iv) actively participating in the community by sponsoring fundraising events or establishing a meaningful local presence.

In essence, philanthropic responsibility underscores the commitment to not only succeed as a business entity but to actively contribute to the betterment of society, fostering a positive and impactful relationship between the company and the community it serves.

Ethical responsibility emphasizes the commitment to fair and ethical conduct. This encompasses several key aspects such as (i) ensuring equitable treatment for all customers, irrespective of age, race, culture, or sexual orientation, (ii) fostering a positive and inclusive environment for employees, transcending personal differences, and providing favorable compensation and benefits that exceed mandated minimums, (iii) promoting diversity in vendor selection by engaging with suppliers of various races, genders, veteran statuses, and economic backgrounds, and (iv) maintaining transparent and timely communication with investors, disclosing operating concerns honestly and respectfully.

Financial responsibility serves as the linchpin that unites the three aforementioned areas. While a company may aspire to elevate its environmental, ethical, and philanthropic focus, the realization of these aspirations' hinges on strategic financial commitments. This involves allocating resources towards (i) research and development for innovative products that promote sustainability, (ii) recruiting a diverse array of talent to foster an inclusive workforce, (iii) initiatives that educate and train employees on diversity, equity, inclusion, social awareness, and environmental concerns, (iv) implementing processes that may incur higher costs but lead to more impactful CSR outcomes, and (v) ensuring transparent and timely financial reporting, including external audits.

In some corporate social responsibility models, there is a shift away from financial responsibility towards a sense of volunteerism. However, the understanding remains that financial investments are instrumental in transforming CSR aspirations into tangible, positive impacts on the environment, society, and ethical practices.

The **main benefits of CSR** are

- brand recognition
- employee engagement
- risk mitigation
- financial success.

Indeed, as a company engages more in CSR, it is more likely to receive favorable **brand recognition**. Customers are increasingly becoming more aware of the impacts companies can have on their community, and many now base purchasing decisions on the CSR aspect of a business. Consumers are then more likely to act favorably toward a company that has acted to benefit its customers as opposed to companies that have demonstrated an ability to deliver quality products.

Workers are also **more likely to stick around a company** that they believe in. This in turn reduces employee turnover, disgruntled workers, and the total cost of a new employee.

Embracing CSR practices enables companies to proactively manage and **mitigate risks** by steering clear of potentially problematic scenarios. Actions such as discrimination against employee groups, neglect of natural resources, or unethical use of company funds have the potential to result in lawsuits, litigation, or legal proceedings, posing financial harm and subjecting the company to negative news headlines. By adhering to CSR principles, companies can safeguard themselves against these risks, fostering a resilient and ethically sound business environment.

For companies looking to get an edge and **outperform the market**, enacting CSR strategies tends to improve how investors feel about an organization and how they view the worth of the company. In a study by Boston Consulting Group, companies that are considered leaders in environmental, social, or governance matters had an 11% valuation premium over their competitors.

There is no universally applicable rubric for assessing the CSR of all companies, as different sources employ diverse criteria when compiling rankings. These evaluations typically consider factors such as employee relations, environmental impact, human rights, governance, and financial decisions.

However, strategically evaluating CSR strategies can pose challenges, as not all benefits are easily quantifiable in financial terms for the company. For instance, assessing the positive impact on a company's brand image resulting from initiatives like planting one million trees may prove intricate due to the subjective nature of brand perception and its financial translation.

The one thing

In the comedy City Slickers, there is a memorable scene where Curly, the old cow-boy played by the late **Jack Palance**, has this profound conversation about life with Mitch, played by **Billy Crystal**.

Curly: Do you know what the secret of life is?

Mitch: No. What?

Curly: This. (holding up one finger)

Mitch: Your finger?

Curly: One thing. Just one thing. You stick to that and everything else don't mean sh*t.

Mitch: That's great, but what is the "one thing"?

Curly: That is what you have got to figure out.

In the following chapters, we will explore the main critical success factors for a successful organization through one specific angle, one thing: **meta-leadership**.

While writing this book, my goal was not to present an exhaustive approach of the topic but rather to identify critical aspects that are the difference that will make the difference, especially in the context of CSR.

Chapter 1 summary

Sustainability requires that companies incorporate social, environmental, and economic considerations into the overall management.

Corporate Social Responsibility (CSR) is a continuous improvement framework designed to that aim.

A modern organization needs to be both stable and agile as the world is now much more interconnected (thus interdependent) and that things can evolve much faster than before, with both more challenges and opportunities out there.

2 - BEYOND LEADERSHIP

"Leadership is a potent combination of strategy and character.
But if you must be without one, be without the strategy."

- Norman Schwarzkopf

The main differentiator for greatness

The word *leadership* comes from the Old English *lithan*, meaning *to go or to travel* (as opposed to *having power or control*). Leadership is therefore about *going first* and influencing others by one's actions and words.

In his bestseller book *Good to Great*, former Stanford business professor **Jim Collins** presents the results of a 5-year study on what differentiates 11 excellent companies from their direct and indirect competitors.

The subject of the research can be summarized as follows: can a good company become excellent and if so, how? His conclusions are both well-founded and interesting.

Of note, criteria that must be met by a company to be considered as excellent are both

- cumulative equity earnings that had not exceeded the market for 15 years and

- a transition point followed by cumulative earnings that were at least three times the market for the next 15 years.

You may ask why 15 years? Because that is, according to **Jim Collins**, a duration that transcends the odds and ends, and exceeds the average duration of most CEO positions. The choice of 3x market value comes from the fact that it exceeds the results of the most widely recognized large companies.

And guess what... the **number one success factor** that made the difference between good and great companies was the **leader's personality**.

Jim Collins and his team define 5 levels of leadership:

- level 1: highly capable individual
- level 2: active team member
- level 3: competent leader
- level 4: effective leader
- level 5: great leader

All excellent companies were characterized by a level 5 leader who demonstrated sustained excellence through a subtle combination of personal humility and professional drive. Examples of such leaders are **Colman Mockler**, CEO of Gillette from 1975 to

1991, and **Abraham Lincoln**, 16th president of the United States from 1861 until his assassination in 1865.

A key point of these leaders is that they also knew how to put in place **successors** capable of perpetuating success. In contrast, in the comparison companies, three out of four leaders installed weak and/or failed successors.

A leadership culture

Robust and sustainable teams and organizations are therefore built on an **empowered leadership culture** as opposed to a cult formed around a particular leader.

In a **cult**, the organization mostly exists and succeeds because of the leader's character. A cult is therefore **rudimentary** and **ephemeral** as it fades away when the leader leaves. A major drawback of cults is the perception of fundamental inequality between people. Indeed, such organizations are based upon a **hierarchy** in which people above are inherently better than those at other levels. This leads to the feeling that people are dispensable entities that can be easily replaced when the lemon has been fully squeezed.

On the contrary, a leadership culture is **much more durable and robust** than a cult as it does not depend so much on the leader alone. Culture is shared by all the members of the organization. It is based on common **purpose/vision, mission, values, beliefs, behavior,** and **knowledge** that can be transmitted to succeeding generations.

Culture is one of the secrets that led the famous **All Blacks** to the top, making them one of the most titled teams in the world. What matters for the All blacks is to leave the jersey a better position. In a broader sense, this means that their main responsibility is to be a good ancestor. Their culture is their legacy.

In a culture, while there are still symbolic individuals who have key responsibilities, people are essentially viewed as **equals** who are in different roles. Roles are based on the development of individual capabilities and are not a reflection of the intrinsic value of the person. As a result, all members are acknowledged and seen as **valuable and indispensable contributors**.

In a culture of leadership, everyone is encouraged to express their ideas and visions openly and honestly. They are not repressed when their opinion differs from their n+1. They are not categorized in subjective Gaussian curves.

In summary, if a leader's success is based on the power of their personality, their job is only half-done.

Nowadays, there is an **increasing need for authentic and conscious leadership**. This includes the way we lead ourselves, our families, our teams, and our businesses. To achieve more in the world, we must first grow, evolve, and **expand our consciousness** personally.

Human needs

There are many theories aimed at explaining why we do what we do. The simplest and most powerful one I know, and personally use in my coaching practice, is **Tony Robbins'** six human needs approach. It also helps to better understand our **emotions** for better relationships and thus a better quality of life.

Indeed, emotions are what drive you to action, hence their name (energy in motion, E-motion). Overall, we all seek to move towards **pleasure** and away from **pain**.

According to **Tony Robbins**, there are 6 universal human needs that you absolutely must satisfy to achieve this goal:

- **certainty**: the assurance of avoiding pain and gaining pleasure (other names can be used such as routine, security, control)

- **uncertainty**: the need for the unknown, change, variety, new stimuli

- **significance**: the need to feel unique, important, special, or necessary

- **love and connection**: the need for a strong sense of closeness or bond with someone or something

- **growth**: the need for the expansion of

capabilities, skills, or understanding, and

- **contribution**: the need to have a sense of service and to focus on helping, giving, and supporting others.

When your needs are not met, you experience unpleasant emotions:

- **anxiety** when you lack certainty

- **boredom** when you lack variety

- **low self-esteem** or **contempt from others** when you lack significance

- **loneliness** when you lack love and connection

- **frustration** when you lack growth and

- **emptiness** or lack of meaning when you lack contribution.

Humans are resourceful and can find many means (**vehicles**) to satisfy their needs; some are healthy, and some are not, as we often seek immediate gratification instead of thinking long-term.

Take importance, for example: you can feel important by constantly talking about yourself or belittling others, or you can satisfy this need by developing yourself and bringing value to others.

The need for connection can be satisfied by creating meaningful relationships and helping others, or by smoking, drinking, or overeating (connecting with oneself).

In reality, things are often much more nuanced, but you get what I mean.

These vehicles should ideally be linked to your **values**. These are fundamental judgments of an ethical, moral, or practical nature that you hold about what really matters to you, what is valuable to you in essence. They constitute a set of beliefs about what you consider right or wrong in your life, and reasons you give yourself to believe that life is worth living. Many people do not have a clear idea of what they consider important. On the other hand, successful people always have a very clear vision of what they consider important.

Once the vehicles are identified, it is interesting to think about the **rules** to follow. Suppose you want to nourish your need for growth by growing your business (your vehicle). What do you need to be satisfied: 10% more customers? 1000% more?

The stricter your rules are, the harder it will be for you to be successful. A healthy way to proceed is to **gradually raise the bar** higher and higher instead of focusing solely on unattainable goals.

Now that you know the 6 human needs and the emotions you feel when they are not met, you have probably identified the 2 needs that are most important to you. These 2 **primary needs** determine your life. If you give more importance to certainty than anything else, your life will be completely different than if you prioritize love first.

We all have the six needs, and all are important, but the ranking matters more in terms of joy and fulfillment. So, if you want to change your life, focus more on love, growth, and contribution.

If you are in a **relationship**, try to meet your needs and those of your partner based on each other's respective vehicles and rules. Also, keep in mind that you are responsible for meeting your own needs and not just wait for the other person to do it for you.

Living values

There are two types of values: the **move-towards** and **move-away** values (the anti-values in other words).

The first ones lead us towards **pleasure** and the second away from **pain**, pleasure and pain being the top driving forces of human beings. as mentioned earlier.

Both types of values are critical as we all want to both avoid pain and get pleasure. One without the other will definitely impair fulfillment.

Within an organization, the move-towards will help you materialize your vision through your mission. The move-away values will help you define what will not be acceptable in terms of attitude and behaviors.

Another distinction can be made between **instrumental** and **intrinsic** (or core) values. Instrumental values are a means to an end (wealth for example) whereas intrinsic values are an end in and of itself (such as happiness). Instrumental values are therefore those we take on, often on a temporary basis, in order to achieve something to support our intrinsic values.

Being able to distinguish between both is critical to clarify and prioritize the values that will lead us to our goals without conflict of values that can emerge when instrumental values produce actions that are not aligned with intrinsic values.

Aligning and bridging values when needed is therefore a critical component of leadership.

Self- & meta-leadership

You are the most important person in your life. Leadership starts therefore with yourself.

Self-leadership is deeply connected with self-mastery and the ability of letting go.

Keep in mind that the results that you get always depend on the way you feel (your **energy**), the way you think (your **mindset**) and the way you take action (your **performance**).

Learn how to master these three pillars and your self-leadership will dramatically increase. For further information, please refer to my previous book *When the impossible becomes possible - the path to self-mastery and letting go*, available on Amazon.

Meta-leadership is the ability to lead other leaders by inspiring them to share a common passion and purpose. It is based upon envisioning a bright future, committing to it, awakening that vision in others and working together with them to make it happen.

Therefore, meta-leadership results from inspiration and engagement, rather than from power.

Meta-goals

According to **Robert Dilts'** modeling of successful

ventures, there are 5 meta-goals of next gen entrepreneurs and leaders that perfectly align with CSR:

- growing personally & spiritually
- contributing to society and the environment
- building a sustainable venture and career
- supporting the emotional and physical wellbeing of oneself and others
- sharing vision and resources with a community of peers, igniting new possibilities.

The 4 goals of meta-leadership to reach these 5 meta goals are therefore:

- achieving results
- promoting change
- developing results
- realizing values.

The meta-leader should hence display qualities such as authenticity, emotional intelligence, purposiveness, and responsibility/accountability.

The 7 Strategies of Successful Genius (according again to **Robert Dilts**' modeling work), will greatly contribute to meta-leadership:

- formulating and communicating a clear and meaningful vision for the future

- maintaining a focus on higher purpose

- influencing through inspiration

- balancing self-interest and the common good, in themselves and others

- respecting and integrating multiple perspectives

- practicing congruence - leading by example (walking the talk)

- exercising mindful self-leadership and reflecting thoughtfully on the lessons gained from experience.

Meta-leadership allows other team members to be leaders, proactive and willing to take responsibility and action. On the contrary, it is not constantly controlling others and telling them what to do.

Meta-leadership **empowers** people to act quickly and flexibly, which can only happen with proper company **culture** and **structure**, which will be discussed in the following chapters.

Empowerment is also directly correlated to the quality of **training** that you can offer to your team members.

Chapter 2 summary

The number one success factor that makes the difference between good and great companies is the leader's personality.

There is an increasing need for authentic and conscious leadership in the world. Aligning needs - the driving force explaining why we do what we do - and values is beneficial for a culture of leadership.

Leadership starts with oneself. Self-leadership is deeply connected with self-mastery and the ability of letting go.

Meta-leadership is the ability to lead other leaders by inspiring them to share a common passion and purpose. It is based upon envisioning a bright future, committing to it, awakening that vision in others and working together with them to make it happen. Meta-leadership results from inspiration and engagement, rather than from power.

Meta-leadership empowers people to act quickly and flexibly, which can only happen with proper company culture and structure. Meta goals and success strategies contribute to meta-leadership.

3 - EMPOWERMENT

"Better people make better All Blacks."

- Graham Henry

According to Google's English dictionary, **empowerment** is both the authority or power given to someone to do something, and the process of becoming stronger and more confident, especially in controlling one's life and claiming one's rights.

Creating other empowered leaders (and not only simply obedient followers) is essential for achieving effective performance and ultimately the survival of an organization, especially in a more interconnected and fast-moving environment.

In his book *Team of Teams*, General **Stanley McChrystal** highlights the importance of empowering team members when speed of action is required.

When he took command of the Joint Task Force in Iraq in 2003 to fight against AQI (Al Qaeda in Iraq), **McChrystal** quickly realized that conventional military tactics were no longer adequate and that he had consequently to adapt his leadership style. At some point, going through the chain of command was too slow. He then made the decision to empower soldiers on the battlefield to act on the spot as speed of action was critical for success.

Now, let's be super clear here: empowerment only works if empowered people do have the **capabilities** to make the decision and/or to perform the task.

Adequate **training and coaching** are therefore critical for success. Interestingly, the percentage of training is usually quite low in the business world, when compared to sports or the military. Interesting, isn't it? More on these topics below.

Deliberate practice

The best illustration I know of deliberate practice is the story of the United States Navy Fighter Weapons School popularized by the movie Top Gun, starring **Tom Cruise**.

During the Vietnam War, the performance of American pilots had dropped to 1 enemy aircraft shot down for every 1 American aircraft, which was not very cost-effective, neither in terms of human lives nor financially (given the cost of a fighter jet). The Americans then implemented deliberate practice, resulting in a ratio of 12 enemy aircraft shot down for every American aircraft between 1970 and 1973. During the 7 months of the first Gulf War, American pilots shot down 33 enemy aircraft in aerial combat, losing only one aircraft during the operation, making it probably the most striking performance in the history of aerial combat.

But what does this famous deliberate practice consist of, you may ask? First, it involves selecting **recognized experts** in their field (here, seasoned veteran pilots) and putting the apprentices (who have also undergone a selection process) in conditions as close as possible to the reality of the field. Then, each practical session is followed by a **debriefing** that highlights the behaviors that worked well and those that need to be improved. Gradually, the students gain both **competence** and **confidence**, which is very well illustrated in the movie.

Deliberate practice is the **key to the success** of World Champions in various fields such as chess, music, and sports.

The number of hours of practice, in other words, training, is obviously important, but it is above all the quality of it that will make the difference.

Building habits & skills

Whatever your goals or the principles and strategies you wish to apply, they will only materialize if you establish the corresponding habits. By habit, I mean a behavior that has been repeated enough to become **automatic**.

It is up to you to establish better habits day after day, week after week, month after month, year after year.

What is fantastic is that our habits are somewhat like **mobile applications**; we can delete them, update them, or even download new ones.

If you want to improve your life or business, you must improve your habits... constantly. This brings us back to the notion of **training**. This is how you will gradually and exponentially gain efficiency and productivity in the areas that truly matter to you. To save time, you can obviously draw inspiration from the habits of successful people, especially if they have already achieved what you want to accomplish.

Here are some important points to help you:

- switch to **discovery** mode

It's a bit like exploring the app store on your smartphone or tablet. You might discover one that you hadn't thought of but that will be particularly useful to you.

- **refresh** your habits regularly

Update your "applications", for example, once a month, quarter, or year.

- establish a system to **measure** the effectiveness of your habits

You will thus know which ones are the most effective and/or best suited to you.

- be clear about your **limits**

For example, what is the maximum weight you are willing to reach? How many consecutive days without exercise do you want to tolerate?

- **adjust** what needs to be based on the results obtained and your living conditions

You can, for example, accept to lower certain criteria if you have to deal with more challenges or workload temporarily. Even the Formula 1 World Champion does not constantly drive at maximum speed. Adaptation is crucial!

But how do you actually establish a better habit? According to **James Clear**, it involves using a 4-step model: the cue, craving, response, and reward.

- **the cue**

This is what **stimulates** your nervous system to initiate a behavior in order to obtain a reward.

- **the craving**

This is the motivation behind every habit. Without **motivation** or desire, you have no reason to act. Cravings differ from person to person and are not triggered by the same signals for everyone. Self-discipline also comes into play at this stage.

- **the response**

This is the **habit itself**, which can take the form of a thought or an action. The response only occurs if you are motivated enough and if you encounter little friction. The response also depends on your skills (see below).

- **the reward**

This is the ultimate goal of each habit, **satisfying** your cravings and teaching you what works best.

To establish a **new habit**, it is ideal to act simultaneously on each of these steps, by making the action both:

- **obvious** (to favor the trigger),
- **attractive** (to create desire),
- **easy** to accomplish (to provide a result), and
- **enjoyable** (to encourage repetition).

Conversely, to get rid of a **bad habit,** you will need to make it both:

- as **invisible** as possible (to avoid the trigger),
- **unattractive** (to decrease the craving),

- **difficult** (to interfere with the response), and
- **unpleasant** (so that there is no reward).

According to various authors, the duration of establishing a new habit takes an average of 66 days (between 18 and 254 days) depending on the habit being established. It can therefore be very quick.

Keep in mind that a little is better than nothing and opt for **progressiveness**. Therefore, make sure that your new habit does not take more than 2 minutes at the beginning so that it is very easy to establish. For example, "reading before bed" will initially be "reading one page". You can then increase the duration. I will conclude this section with 3 tips that will guarantee the establishment of new habits:

- **stack** them on other existing habits,
- **adapt** them to your environment (and vice versa),
- follow and **measure** them.

No matter what habits we put in place to achieve our dreams, they will only be effective if we are competent in their implementation.

According to **Robert B. Dilts** & **Mickey A. Feher**, our skills are generally evaluated based on 3 dimensions:
- whether we enjoy doing the action or not,
- whether we do it well and
- whether we spend time on it.

If you tick all three boxes, and your actions are in line with your passion, mission, and ambition, then you are in your **zone of genius.** That is what you should aim for.

If you tick all three boxes, but your actions are not entirely in line with your passion, mission, and ambition, then you are in your **zone of excellence**. If you do not spend time on it, you are in an **unexploited zone of excellence.**

If you do the activity well and spend time on it but do not enjoy it, you are in your **competence zone**. If you don't spend time on it, you are in an **unexploited competence zone**.

If you enjoy the activity, spend time on it, but are not particularly good at it, it is more like a **hobby**.
If you enjoy the activity but are not particularly good

at it and don't dedicate much time to it, it is an **interest**.

If you spend time doing something you neither enjoy nor do well, you are in the **incompetence zone**.

If you don't check any of the boxes, the activity will be a **waste of time** for you.

Keep in mind that these 3 dimensions are **interconnected**; the more you enjoy something, the more likely you are to spend time on it and become good at it (if you apply deliberate practice). And the more time you spend and become good at it, the more you will probably enjoy it. Therefore, it can be useful to train to become better and plan practice time to progress (consistency before quantity).

We experience **maximum motivation** when we work on tasks that are at the limits of our current abilities. Not too difficult. Not too easy. Just right.

Smart feedback

In *The new one minute manager*, **Ken Blanchard** and **Spencer Johnson** are sharing two essential tips for supporting deliberate practice with proper feedback.

When training or working towards clear goals, people might indeed either succeed or fail.

The idea is to help them reach their full potential by catching them doing something right. In other words, it consists in giving praisings as much as possible when they succeed, especially when starting a new job or project. Adequate praisings helps people get confidence and hence further take initiatives when speed of action or innovation is required. The magic of this is that it could be done in one minute according to the following process:

- 30 sec to praise by being specific on what people did right and to mention how it makes you feel,

- a short pause to allow people to feel good about what they have done and

- the rest of the minute to encourage them to

do more of the same and highlight your confidence in them.

When people fail or have done something wrong and need to get back on track to achieve their goals, they should be redirected as soon as possible. The process is also quite simple:

- review the facts and be super specific

- mention how you feel and what the impact on the results might be

- pause a few seconds to let sink in

- remind that you trust and value your employee and

- realize that when the redirect is over, it is over.

In brief, when people succeed, you praise them so that they will proceed with more success. When they lose, you redirect them so that they will proceed with better performance. In both cases, you win.

Why talent is overrated

These days, we hear a lot about the talent shortage. But what is talent and is it really the key factor?

American psychologist **Carol S. Dweck** has devoted her career to studying mindset, which she differentiates between a **fixed mindset** and a **growth mindset**. In her book *Mindset: The New Psychology of Success*, she explains, with numerous examples from her research findings, anecdotes from everyday life, and biographical elements of famous personalities, how having a mindset oriented towards learning and continuous improvement (the growth mindset) leads to a much richer life in terms of success and fulfillment in all areas (education, social and romantic relationships, sports, business).

Do you think your intelligence is an innate trait that you can't really change? Do you believe you cannot change essential components of your personality? If you answered *yes*, you most likely have a fixed mindset. If, on the contrary, you believe that, regardless of your level of intelligence, you can improve it, and change certain aspects of your personality, then you definitely have a growth mindset.

Michael Jordan wasn't a natural born athlete, but he was one of the hardest workers in the history of sports. He was cut from his high school varsity basketball team, not recruited by the University of North Carolina, his dream school, and not drafted by the first two NBA teams that could have picked him. When he was cut from the varsity team, he was devastated. But he got in the habit of leaving home at 6am to practice before school. At the University of North Carolina, he constantly worked on his weaknesses. Even at the height of his glory, his relentless training was legendary. For him, success comes from the mindset. Champions are not born, they are made.

Of course, we all have both mindsets, perhaps one more than the other, and perhaps differently depending on the areas of our lives (health, finances, love, work...).

Skills and talent alone are not enough. The most important thing to face and overcome challenges is to approach them with a growth mindset.

So, when building your team, think beyond a resume and assess as much as possible the individual **potential**, then invest in them through appropriate **development & training plans** including deliberate practice.

Mitigating the risks

Empowerment can sometimes go too far when people are neither trained nor supported enough. This can lead to exhaustion, burn-out or even dramatic outcomes such as civilian massacres in war zones.

The proper way to mitigate the risks is to ensure that a strong **governance** is in place and available before any potential issue if possible and after in any case. This will allow you to take responsibility for what happened and deal with the consequences as best as you can, as well as to avoid any recurrence by learning from your mistakes and strengthening when needed.

In complex environments and/or organizations, I recommend a **cross-functional** governance which will ensure both efficient decision-making and **cross-fertilization** between key stakeholders. More on that later.

Chapter 3 summary

Creating other empowered leaders (and not only simply obedient followers) is essential for achieving effective performance in a more interconnected and fast-moving environment.

The percentage of training is usually quite low in the business world, when compared to sports or the military.

Deliberate practice will allow the appropriate development of habits and hence competencies that are needed for efficient empowerment.

Smart feedback is critical. When people succeed, you praise them so that they will proceed with more success. When they lose, you redirect them so that they will proceed with better performance. In both cases, you win.

Growth mindset outperforms talent.

A cross-functional governance will help mitigate the risks linked to empowerment.

4 - GENERATIVE TEAMWORK

"The whole is greater than the sum of its parts."

- Aristotle

Collective intelligence

Collective intelligence is a shared intelligence that emerges from the **collaboration** and **communication** between individuals in teams, groups, or organizations.

Its **main benefits** are

- wiser decisions
- new ideas and creative solutions
- enhanced performance.

Collective intelligence is a consequence of people working cooperatively to reach **common visions and ambitions** by constantly exchanging **information** and **ideas**, and by complementing and synergizing one another's **skills, experience, and imagination**.

Therefore, a successful teamwork implies **win-win interactions** where everyone benefits in some way and where the whole is greater than the sum of its parts. Win-win interactions create a positively **self-reinforcing feedback loop** that produces co-evolution and growth.

According to **Robert Dilts**' work on modeling successful organizations, collective intelligence is produced by three fundamental dynamics: resonance, synergy and emergence.

Resonance denotes a form of mutual influence between entities, be they objects, systems, or people, wherein they are particularly attuned and exhibit stronger vibrations at specific frequencies. In group dynamics, resonance occurs when members experience a profound **alignment** and **connection** with the ideas, values, and goals of their fellow group members. Both intellectual and emotional resonance play a pivotal role in fostering motivation and synergy within the group.

Synergy occurs when two or more things function together to produce a result that is not independently obtainable by any of the things on their own. It is the ability of a team, group, or organization to **outperform even its best individual member** and produce better results than if each member were working individually.

Emergence happens when something new arises out of interactions between different elements in a system. A robust emergence takes place when the outcomes of collective behavior cannot be directly attributed to individual components but rather to their intricate interactions. In such cases, the entirety becomes distinctly **greater than the mere sum of its parts**. Emergence serves as a paradigmatic lens, exploring phenomena ranging from the intricate beauty of a snowflake to the organizational structure of ant colonies and the dynamics of economic markets.

The **fundamental principle** of emergence is **1+1=3**, which is characteristic of a high-performing group. In contrast, the performance in an underperforming group is $1+1<2$ and the one in an average group is $1+1=2$.

Dynamic teaming

Dynamic teaming involves integrating different competencies and personal traits in a way that each team member is **clear** about the **purpose, roles, and responsibilities** as well as **operating principles** of the team.

With dynamic teaming, even a small number of people with complementary skills, common purpose, **mutual accountability,** and **collective responsibility** can achieve remarkable results.

In his book *Generative collaboration*, **Robert Dilts** shares the example where a team of 20 people outperformed a team of 1,000 people to develop a product for a very important segment of the telecommunications market.

The team of 1,000 people operated in **silos** largely isolated from one another where the various team members simply worked to carry out the task that they had been assigned by the project leader, who viewed people as essentially parts of a machine or computer software program.

On the contrary, the smaller team was led by a person who was passionate about the vision for the project and **spread** that **passion** to his team. This leader operated much more as an orchestrator of innovation and encouraged the team to be in **constant communication and interaction**, challenging, stimulating, and supporting each other to be and give the best of themselves, **think outside the box** and reach for excellence in everything they did. They were able to achieve a high level of generative collaboration, stimulating and supporting one another to move forward in new ways and **create something unprecedented**.

A similar lesson can be learned from history and in particular from the **Battle of Midway**. In early June 1942, a huge Japanese fleet under the command of Admiral **Isoroku Yamamoto** headed to the Midway islands in the Central Pacific to secure the islands and launch base for an invasion of Hawaii.

Though outnumbered by more than 18-to-1, the American forces under the command of Admiral **Chester W. Nimitz** won the battle due their capacity for dynamic teaming.

The difference that made the difference is that **Nimitz** made no attempt to direct the battle, but instead established simple rules of communication between fighter pilots:

- keep all radio channels to other planes open

- listen but say nothing unless you are

    - coming under attack from enemy fighters
    - in a position to attack an enemy ship.

By making the rules simple and clear, **Nimitz** empowered his pilots and generated powerful and self-organizing dynamics among the American planes.

Similar to the above example of the team of 20 people, the Battle of Midway was won not through the assembly of superior force, but by a brilliant **meta-leader** who empowered his team members and favored dynamic teaming by trust and freedom to operate with **clear and simple rules**.

To summarize, teams form along the dimensions of both

- **relationship** (persons associated together) and
- **task** (their work or activity).

Dynamic team development involves facilitating both of these aspects, i.e. respectively

- encouraging or strengthening relationships
- defining and clarifying tasks, and the competencies and actions necessary to accomplish those tasks.

Psychological safety

As the activities of organizations become increasingly complex and global, the majority of what it takes to be successful is more and more team based.

Google also realized that analyzing and improving individual workers - known as *employee performance optimisation* wasn't enough. As a result, they became focused on building the **perfect team**. They looked at 180 teams from all over the company, gathering and analyzing lots of data. Nothing was showing that the *who* part of the equation mattered. Instead, they identified two characteristics that all good teams seemed to share.

First, members spoke in roughly the same proportion, that is, each person had **equal opportunity to contribute**. As long as everyone got a chance to talk, the team did well. But if one person or a small group spoke all the time, the collective intelligence declined.

Secondly, members of good teams all had a high degree of **social sensitivity**, meaning that they were skilled at perceiving how others felt based on their tone of voice, facial expressions, and other nonverbal cues. This capacity is an expression of **empathy and emotional intelligence**. It also relates to the ability to take on someone else's point of view.

The combination of both traits produces what is known as **psychological safety**, which is a sense of confidence that the team will not embarrass, reject, or punish someone for speaking up. It describes a team climate characterized by interpersonal **trust** and **mutual respect** in which people are comfortable being themselves. According to Google's data, psychological safety, more than anything else, was critical to making a teamwork. Psychological safety is also promoted by authentic self-disclosure, where people can share what they genuinely think and feel and are able to reveal intimate information about themselves.

Another factor that emerges from the Google study was the importance of **perceived task significance**. In effective teams, the group members knew their work fit into Google's larger mission. Task significance is the result of a person's **awareness and understanding** of the extent their results affect the organization. The greater they are, the higher the impact on results.

Therefore, the combination of **psychological safety** and **task significance** encourages and allows team members to be both separate wholes as well as act as part of something larger.

Full engagement

According to the NYT bestselling author **Shirzad Chamine**, only 20% of individuals and teams reach their full potential.

Why are New Year's resolutions often forgotten after a few weeks? Why do people who want to lose weight engage in yo-yo diets? Why do we so quickly abandon what we learn in training?

It is because we unconsciously **self-sabotage**. The consequence is not only an impact on the expression of our potential but also a considerable loss of time and energy.

Our **inner judge** is our greatest saboteur, especially since we are rarely fully aware of its existence and importance.

Judging or criticizing others, external conditions, or yourself (or all three) is indeed probably the most important failure strategy that impacts both our motivation and our full engagement. It often comes into play when you don't feel happy, that is, when your current living conditions are not aligned with your ideal. It will be much more profitable to **take responsibility** and take action where you can and let go where you cannot act.

In his book *Positive Intelligence*, **Chamine** describes 9 accomplice saboteurs:

- the Avoider,
- the Controller,
- the Hyper-Achiever,
- the Hyper-Rational,
- the Hyper-Vigilant,
- the Pleaser,
- the Restless,
- the Stickler and
- the Victim.

These saboteurs are universal because they are connected to areas of our brain linked to our survival. We develop them in early childhood to survive the physical and emotional threats we perceive at that time, through our child's eyes. They are no longer useful to us as adults, although they remain present without our knowledge.

You can identify the most important ones for you on the website https://www.positiveintelligence.com/saboteurs.

Chamine also identifies **5 sages** in particular to serve as antidotes:

- the **empathizer** (compassion and understanding towards others and yourself),

- the **explorer** (curiosity and open-mindedness),

- the **innovator** (new perspectives and solutions),

- the **navigator** (the path most aligned with your values and mission), and

- the **activator** (taking action without being disturbed by the saboteurs).

Engaging in a **mental fitness training** plan that will help you decrease your self-sabotage, and that of your team members is one of my main advices to reach your next level.

Chapter 4 summary

Collective intelligence is a shared intelligence that emerges from the collaboration and communication between individuals in teams, groups, or organizations. It is produced by three fundamental dynamics: resonance, synergy, and emergence.

A successful teamwork implies win-win interactions where everyone benefits in some way and where the whole is greater than the sum of its parts.

Dynamic teaming involves integrating different competencies and personal traits in a way that each team member is clear about the purpose, roles, and responsibilities as well as operating principles of the team.

A brilliant meta-leader empowers his team members and favors dynamic teaming by trust and freedom to operate with clear and simple rules.

The combination of psychological safety and task significance encourages and allows team members to be both separate wholes as well as act as part of something larger.

Only 20% of individuals and teams reach their full potential due to self-sabotage. Engaging in a mental fitness training plan will help you decrease your self-sabotage, and that of your team members.

5 - STRUCTURAL FRAMEWORK

"Diversity is a fact. Inclusion is a choice."

- Timothy R. Clark

Scientific management

The notion of top-down, rigidly predetermined, scientific management of behavior in the civilian sector is largely the legacy of the nineteenth-century **Frederick Winslow Taylor**. Taylor was a habitual optimizer by nature and made more, faster, with less.

Determined to be as scientific as possible in his optimizing, he followed the reductionist impulses of classical mechanics, breaking every job down to its most granular elements. The small gains made by optimizing each tiny element came together to make a substantial difference in efficiency.

Taylor's methods were cruel, but, for business owners, his results were undeniable in terms of **profits**. Taylor's ideas spread from company to company and from industry to industry, and his success represented the legitimization of **management** as a discipline.

Managers assumed dual roles as both research scientists and architects of efficiency, delineating a clear **boundary** between thought and action. The managerial domain became one of contemplation and planning, while workers were tasked solely with execution. This shift relieved them of the expectation to comprehend the intricacies of how and why things functioned, significantly altering their perception of **task significance**. As explored in the preceding chapter, this change resulted in the loss of a crucial element contributing to long-term fulfillment and performance.

In the decades since, **Taylor**'s star has dimmed. His treatment of workers has been widely decried, as his conception of individuals as mechanistic entities to be manipulated.

While we may cringe at the harsh repercussions of the dehumanizing conditions experienced on assembly lines in the past, the principles that formed the foundation of these systems persistently influence the approaches organizations of all kinds take towards management and leadership. The pursuit of an optimal method, the steadfast belief in organizational leaders as planners, synchronizers, and coordinators - akin to chess-player strategists overseeing interconnected military troop movements, marketing initiatives, or global supply chains - remains deeply ingrained in our collective mindset.

However, the technological changes of recent decades have led to a **more interdependent and fast-paced world**. This creates a state of **complexity** that produces a fundamentally different situation from the complicated challenges of the past; complicated problems required great effort, but ultimately yielded to prediction. Complexity means that, in spite of our increased abilities to track and measure, the world has become, in many ways, vastly less predictable. This **unpredictability** is fundamentally incompatible with reductionist managerials models based around planning and prediction. The new environment demands a new approach.

Since the pursuit of efficiency can limit flexibility and resilience, **McChrystal** and his Task Force had to pivot away from seeing efficiency as the managerial holy grail. In the face of a perpetually evolving threat within a complex environment, the imperative was to embrace **adaptability**. The adversary seemed to master this quality through their **networked structure**, capable of dynamic reconfiguration with remarkable **agility and resilience**. To emerge victorious, the Task Force had to transform into a genuine network, mirroring the adaptability required for navigating the challenges they confronted.

They strategically aligned themselves with the principles of **antifragility** as articulated by **Nassim Nicholas Taleb**. Rather than attempting to foresee every conceivable scenario, they focused on identifying and fortifying their vulnerabilities, actively seeking opportunities to enhance their resilience and strength. This proactive approach allowed them to not only withstand unexpected challenges but also transform adversity into opportunities for continuous improvement. By fostering a culture of adaptability and continuous **self-assessment**, they cultivated an organizational ethos that thrived in the face of uncertainty, embodying the essence of antifragility in their pursuit of excellence.

A team of teams

The **MECE** acronym stands for *Mutually Exclusive and Collectively Exhaustive*. A MECE breakdown takes something into a series of categories that do not overlap, but together cover everything. The classic org chart is a neatly MECE structure. The connections that matter are the sparse vertical ones between workers and their managers.

A **non-MECE** structure is much more efficient in sports or where high adaptability is required. A team is better off with the cohesive ability to improvise as a unit, relying on both specialization and overlapping responsibilities, as well as such familiarity with one another's habits and responses that they can anticipate instinctively one another's responses. The best teams know their leader trusts them to **trust** each other. Those horizontal anti-MECE bonds of trust and **overlapping definitions of purpose** enable them to *do the right thing*.

Understanding this difference between MECE and non-MECE structures was a key success factor of **McChrystal**'s Task Force. Being able to connect special forces such as Navy SEALs and Army Rangers with organizations such as CIA, FBI and NSA came from stopping working in silos and adopting a non-MECE structure **much more interconnected** and hence **agile**.

The solution **McChrystal** created was **a team of teams**, an organization within which the relationships between constituent teams resembled those between individuals on a single team: teams that had traditionally resided in separate silos would now have to become fused to one another via trust and purpose.

Of note, this notion of team of teams perfectly defines my vision of **win-win partnerships** or strategic **alliances** where separate enterprises work together towards common goals, sharing success, risks and issues together.

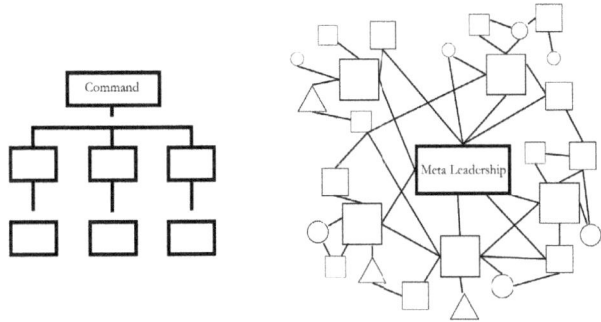

Decentralized governance

Another crucial element of the Joint Task Force transformation to a much more efficient organization was the establishment of a **cross-functional governance meeting**, the Operations and Intelligence (O&I) brief.

It was key to build the **culture of sharing** that they needed to gain in speed, agility and hence effectiveness. Every member of the Task Force, as well as any of the invited partners, was then able to connect. The meeting ran six days a week and included thousands of personnel. By allowing people sharing and sometimes debating perspectives, it gave attendees the **skills and confidence** to better understand the global picture and solve their similar problems without the need for further guidance or clarification. At the end, it saved an incalculable amount of time that was no longer needed to seek clarification or permission.

Shared consciousness in an organization is either hindered or helped by physical spaces and established processes. Often, efforts to facilitate **Taylor**-inspired efficiencies have produced barriers to information sharing and the kind of systemic understanding they needed to pervade the Task Force.

Establishing the necessary transparency and information-sharing at the scale they aspired to demand a comprehensive overhaul, not only of their **physical infrastructure** but also a profound reconsideration of virtually **every procedural aspect** within their organizational culture. The linchpin of this transformative process was the daily O&I briefing, serving as the epicenter for disseminating information across the entire spectrum of their operations to all Task Force members and partner agencies. Moreover, it provided an **inclusive platform**, allowing every individual the opportunity to contribute actively to the collective knowledge pool.

The concept that optimal order emerges not from centralized design but through decentralized interactivity starkly contrasts with the reductive planning methodologies that have historically prevailed in most organizations over the past century. In environments characterized by heightened levels of interaction, ingenious solutions have the potential to organically manifest, transcending the constraints of a single designer or planner. In other words, **order can emerge from the bottom up**, as opposed to being directed, with a plan, from the top down.

Cooperation across silos is necessary for success, which requires building more trust between participants. To this end, the use of **embedding and**

liaison programs creates strong lateral ties between units, and with partner organizations if any. Where systemic understanding mirrors the sense of "purpose" that bonds small teams, this mirrored the second ingredient to team formation: "trust".

Unified by **purpose and trust**, the combination of empowered execution and shared consciousness enables adaptability, allowing for effective responses to the challenges of complexity, characterized by the need for speed and interdependence.

Wisdom of crowds

In addition, groups are remarkably intelligent under the right circumstances.

According to **James Surowiecki** in his book *The wisdom of crowds*, collective decisions are most likely to be good when they are made by people with diverse opinions reaching independent conclusions, relying primarily on their private information.

The **four conditions** that produce wise crowds are

- diversity of opinion (representing a wide range of perspectives)
- independence (people's opinions are not determined by the opinions of those around them)
- decentralization (people can specialize and draw upon local information)
- aggregation (some unbiased mechanism exists for turning individual conclusions into a collective decision).

By adapting his governance, **McChrystal** clearly favored a higher wisdom and hence performance of his team of teams.

A new approval process for key decisions

Tasks inherent in management, such as *planning, organizing, commanding, coordinating, and controlling,* are considerably facilitated with increased access to **information**. This often initiates a cyclical pattern wherein there is a constant pursuit of methods to gather and centralize more information, enabling the formulation and dissemination of progressively efficient directives throughout the organization. In this paradigm, the role of workers becomes instrumental in feeding this cycle, as they await and execute the next set of commands.

When in Iraq, **McChrystal** and his team had simultaneous access to live updates and real-time video from offices and operations across the world and were connected to almost every decision of consequence. They can see that their sharing of information was an effective tool, but the centralization of control that came with such access to tactical data was another question entirely.

As the approval process of key decisions was often slowing down the reactivity on the field, and that often his own advice was not bringing value to what the team on the field would have decided, he communicated across the command his thought process on key decisions such as airstrikes and told them to make the call. He ultimately remained accountable for any decision but empowered his team to what was needed.

The practice of relying decisions up and down the chain of command is premised on the assumption that the organization has the time to do so, or, more accurately, that the cost of the delay is less than the cost of the errors produced by removing a supervisor. In 2004 this assumption no longer held. The risks of acting too slowly were higher than the risks of letting competent people make judgment calls.

The point at which a team suck

As it relates to manpower, there is a point where adding more members to e.g. a team will not bring more value, and eventually even less.

So **how many is too many**? It depends. For tasks such as producing an item on an assembly line, the hundredth employee can add just as much value as the first. For teams, the range is considerably narrower. A soccer team, for instance, consists of eleven players whereas SEAL squads contain between sixteen and twenty people. Beyond such numbers, teams begin to lose the oneness that makes them adaptable. Communication and trust break down, egos come into conflict and innovation and resilience, in other words agility, are affected or lost. The erosion of adaptability can have a profound and far-reaching impact on an organization or business. Remarkably, the very qualities that contribute to the effectiveness of an adaptable team can become a double-edged sword, particularly as organizations expand. The attributes that make a team agile and responsive can sometimes clash with the established structures they are meant to complement.

Thousands of businesses have sunk because of an inability to scale their teamwork, where the **rigidity** that sets in with scale is one of the main causes of start-up failure. Team dynamics are therefore powerful but delicate, and expansion might break them. As a team gets bigger, the number of links that need to be managed among members goes up at an accelerating, almost exponential rate. Bigger teams are therefore not necessarily better than smaller ones because they have more resources to draw on.

Outsourcing is a way to expand its business without directly expanding its workforce with the potential drawbacks highlighted above. A key for success is therefore to consider the partnerships as a team of teams and follow the same principles as **McChrystal** used in Iraq.

Turning the flywheel

When you have defined and set-up your structural framework, you must check its functionality.

In his book *Good to great* cited earlier, **Jim Collins** mentions the **flywheel effect** which he describes in more detail in a separate book. He presents it as one of the major differentiators between excellent companies and their more mediocre competitors.

Imagine your project or company as a steering wheel. You turn it over and over again. At first, it turns very, very slowly and is extremely hard to turn. Then, as you go along, it turns faster and easier. This represents 50% of the flying effect.

But that's not all! You still need to define the steps of your flywheel and the order in which to operate them.

Let's take the example of Amazon. From the very beginning, **Jeff Bezos** had imbued Amazon with an obsession: to create more and more value for more and more customers. He and his team drew the following wheel: low prices lead to more and more visits, which leads to more sales and attracts more third-party sellers who want to sell on the site. The result is that Amazon gets a better return on its fixed costs (servers, storage and delivery centers, etc.). The increased efficiency then allows prices to be pulled down even further. Whichever part of the flywheel is reinforced, it is accelerating and gaining momentum.

The process is shown in the figure below.

Here is a simple 6-steps method to create your own flywheel.

1. Identify ideally up to 6 **critical steps** in your own business. Start with post-it notes to allow flexibility for your brainstorming. Keep it simple.

2. Put them **in the right order**, where each step is influencing the following one. Feel free to try different options.

3. Create secondary flywheels if needed to further describe key steps. This will be highly beneficial to **further dissect** blocking steps and hence unblock them.

4. Share with experts or knowledgeable friends and **get some insights**, especially from people with experience and most of all open-mind and kindness.

5. Then put it to the **test**. Does it work? If so, continue to turn it. If not, figure out if you are not missing any critical step, or if there is a blocking point somewhere.

6. **Repeat** from step 1

Whether the flywheels turn or not, periodically revisiting them offers an opportunity for improvement or adaptation. This reflective practice is particularly valuable in assessing whether adjustments are needed in response to changing environmental factors that may impact your business.

Assessing performance

Measurement is critical to assess where your team or organization stands and how to get even better and grow further.

At individual and even team level, the health of an organization can be measured using the **PQ**, the Positive Intelligence Quotient expressed as a percentage from 0 to 100 (calculable for an individual and for a team). This corresponds to the percentage of time during which your mind serves you instead of sabotaging you. A PQ of 75 indicates that your mind serves you 75% of the time and sabotages you during the remaining 25%. This figure of 75 is not insignificant because it represents the tipping point beyond which you must be positioned to be in evolution and not dragged down. You can measure your PQ by visiting the website https://www.positiveintelligence.com.

To improve your PQ, you *simply* need to learn to **recognize** your saboteurs, **weaken** them, and activate and **strengthen** your sages, the positive counterparts of the saboteurs.

Other simple systems of measurements do exist, such as simple Google forms that allow **anonymous** collection of team member **perceptions and suggestions** of improvement, hence giving them the opportunity to become more involved in the company.

From a more formal perspective, the International Organization for Standardization (ISO) released in 2010 ISO 26000, a set of voluntary standards meant to help companies implement CSR. Unlike other ISO standards, ISO 26000 provides guidance rather than requirements because the nature of CSR is more qualitative than quantitative, and its standards cannot be certified.

ISO 26000 clarifies what CSR is and helps organizations translate CSR principles into practical actions. The standard is aimed at all types of organizations, regardless of their activity, size, or location. And because many key stakeholders from around the world contributed to developing ISO 26000, this standard represents an international consensus.

Chapter 5 summary

The notion of top-down, rigidly predetermined, scientific management is largely the legacy of the nineteenth-century Frederick Winslow Taylor.

However, the technological changes of recent decades have led to a more interdependent and fast-paced world. This creates a state of complexity that produces a fundamentally different situation from the complicated challenges of the past.

A team of teams is an organization within which the relationships between constituent teams resembled those between individuals on a single team: teams that had traditionally resided in separate silos would now have to become fused to one another via trust and purpose.

This can apply to win-win partnerships or strategic alliances where separate enterprises work together towards common goals, sharing success, risks, and issues together.

Groups are remarkably intelligent under the right circumstances. A cross-functional governance meeting is key to build the culture of sharing needed to gain in speed, agility and hence effectiveness. By allowing people sharing and sometimes debating perspectives, it gave attendees the skills and confidence to better understand the global picture and solve their similar problems without the need for further guidance or clarification. At the end, it saved an incalculable amount of time that was no longer needed to seek clarification or permission.

The practice of relying decisions up and down the chain of command is premised on the assumption that the organization has the time to do so, or, more accurately, that the cost of the delay is less than the cost of the errors produced by removing a supervisor.

Beyond such numbers, teams begin to lose the oneness that makes them adaptable. Communication and trust break down, egos come into conflict and innovation and resilience, in other words agility, are affected or lost.

Outsourcing is a way to expand its business without directly expanding its workforce. A key for success is to consider the partnerships as a team of teams.

When you have defined and set-up your structural framework, you must check its functionality by imagining your project or company as a steering wheel. You turn it over and over again. At first, it turns very, very slowly and is extremely hard to turn. Then, as you go along, it turns faster and easier.

Measurement is critical to assess where you stand and how to get even better and grow further. At individual and even team level, the health of an organization can be measured using the Positive Intelligence Quotient (PQ). Other simple systems do exist such as Google forms and from a more formal perspective, the ISO 26000, a set of voluntary standards meant to help companies implement CSR.

6 - CONCLUSION

"A society grows great when old men plant trees in whose shade they know they shall never sit."

Greek proverb

Expanding consciousness

Sustainable development is one of the main challenges the world is facing today. In brief, it consists of actual and future economic growth without prejudicing future generations in any ways. Truly sustainable development implies therefore the capacity to thrive as an individual, a team, an organization, and a society.

Since the Industrial Revolution, most industries have subscribed to management doctrines informed by or similar to **Frederick Taylor**'s scientific management, a system that is excellent for achieving highly efficient execution of known, repeatable processes at scale. Despite the success of this approach throughout the twentieth century, it had its limits. Efficiency is no longer enough.

In order to thrive in our VUCA world, we need to **dynamically adapt** to our environment in a way that uses resources wisely and also makes us **fit for the future**. Prediction is not the only way to confront threats; developing resilience, learning how to reconfigure to confront the unknown, is a much more effective way to respond to a complex environment.

Conscious leadership requires therefore **expanding the scope of consciousness** in multiple dimensions. This is clearly a challenging but important step in our evolution.

A great practice is the Native American notion of **seven generation stewardship** (originated from the Great Law of the Iroquois) which advises people to remember seven generations in the past and consider seven generations in the future when making critical decisions.

Leveraging CSR

Corporate Social Responsibility is a broad concept that can take many forms depending on the company and industry.

It should be seen as a **business model** by which companies make a concerted effort to operate in ways that enhance rather than degrade society and the environment.

CSR initiatives strive to have a **positive impact** on the world through direct benefits to society, nature, and the community in which a business operates.

For example, many companies have taken steps to improve the **environmental sustainability** of their operations, e.g. by installing renewable energy sources or purchasing carbon offsets. In the supply chain, efforts have also been taken to eliminate reliance on unethical labor practices, such as child labor and slavery.

Corporate responsibility programs can also **raise morale** in the workplace. Knowing their company is promoting good causes, employee satisfaction may increase, and retention of staff may be strengthened.

In addition, consumers may be more likely to choose to transact with companies that are attempting to make a more conscious positive impact beyond the scope of its business.

For a company to be socially responsible, it first needs to be **accountable** to itself and beyond. This brings us back to meta-leadership.

Management versus leadership

In businesses and organizations, leadership is still often contrasted with management.

In comparison, leadership is defined as *getting others to want to do things*, while management is typically defined as *getting things done through others*.

Management is usually associated with improving productivity, establishing **order and stability**, and making things run effectively and smoothly.

Leadership is required to **keep moving forward in times of uncertainty**, turbulence, social transformation, and change. When we are in survival mode, we are struggling to maintain business as usual. We are not focused on really growing and flourishing.

Although we intuitively know the world has changed, most leaders reflect a model and leader development process that are sorely **out of date**. We often demand unrealistic levels of knowledge in leaders and force them into ineffective attempts to micromanage.

The temptation to lead as a chess master, controlling each move of the organization to meet the need for certainty, must give way to an approach as a gardener, enabling rather than directing.

Meta-leadership brings simple leadership to another level where other team or organization members are seen not only as resources but as other leaders as well. In my opinion, it brings a higher sense of **inclusion**, **responsibility,** and **sustainable growth**. In other words, it expands consciousness by balancing more **ego** (ourselves) and **soul** (beyond ourselves) according to **Robert Dilts'** definitions.

The **conditions for creating collective intelligence** are a perception of a mutual mission in service of a common vision of benefiting others, the commitment to something larger than oneself, open communication, mutual trust, and respect, as well as curiosity.

Leading by example

Effective adaptation to threats and opportunities requires empowered execution. Individuals and teams closest to the problem offer the best ability to decide and act decisively.

McChrystal was more effective when he supervised processes - from intelligence operations to the prioritization of resources - ensuring avoidance of the silos or bureaucracy that doomed agility, rather than making individual operational decisions.

When he tried to do the same things tighter and faster under the constraints of the old system, his team managed to increase the number of raids from 10 to 18. By 2006, under the new system, this figure skyrocketed to 300! With minimal increases in personnel and funding, they were running **17 times faster**! And these raids were more successful as they were finding a higher percentage of their targets, due in large part to the fact that they were finally moving as fast as AQI, but also because of the increased quality of decision-making.

The move-by-move control that seemed natural to military operations proved less effective than **nurturing the organization** - its structure, processes, and culture - to enable the subordinate components to function with **smart autonomy**. This allowed a constant flow of **shared consciousness** from across the organization, and it freed its members to execute actions in pursuit of the overall strategy as best they saw it.

As in a **garden**, the outcome was less dependent on the initial planting then on consistent maintenance. The gardener cannot actually grow veggies - he can only foster an environment in which the plants do so.

For **McChrystal**, the shift from a heroic leader to a humble gardener was challenging, requiring an adaptation to the new reality. As a leader, he recognized the necessity to transform himself in order to reshape the organization. Despite the changing role, leadership remained more crucial than ever. It evolved into meta-leadership, where his emphasis shifted from manipulating pieces on the board to actively **shaping the entire ecosystem**.

His transformed role was notably characterized by a fundamental shift, focusing on the question: *What do you need?* This marked a departure from traditional leadership styles, where directives were given top-down. Instead, he embraced a **servant-leadership** approach, understanding that effective leadership involved asking his team members about their needs and challenges and then providing the necessary support and resources. This emphasis on tailored support fostered a collaborative and empowered environment, encouraging individual growth and the overall success of the team.

McChrystal also adopted a practice called *thinking out loud*. In this approach, he would encapsulate what he had heard, elucidate his thought process in digesting the information, and articulate his initial considerations on the actions they should contemplate. This method enabled the entire command to trace and, if necessary, amend his logical progression, gaining insights into his decision-making process. Subsequently, in a deliberate move to strengthen empowered execution, he frequently prompted subordinates to independently assess suitable courses of action and communicate their planned initiatives.

Engaging in open, candid thinking can be an intimidating prospect for a senior leader. In such moments, one's lack of knowledge becomes readily apparent, and attempts to feign expertise are usually embarrassingly ineffective. However, **McChrystal** discovered that posing seemingly simple questions or openly admitting "I don't know" was not only accepted but often appreciated. Requesting opinions or seeking advice conveyed a sense of respect. The overarching message conveyed by the O&I, the new cross-functional governance, was that *they* collectively face a challenge that only *them*, as a unified team, can comprehend and solve.

The Task Force transformation is reflective of the new generation of mental models we must adopt in order to make sense of the twenty-first century. If we do manage to embrace this change, we can unlock tremendous potential for human progress.

There are two questions that we have to ask ourselves. The first is "Where am I going?" and the second is "Who will go with me?" - Howard Thurman

Key takeaways

Sustainability in organizations necessitates the integration of social, environmental, and economic considerations into overall management, epitomized by the continuous improvement framework of Corporate Social Responsibility (CSR).

Modern organizations must strike a balance between stability and agility, acknowledging the interconnected nature of the world.

Meta-leadership emerges as a critical catalyst for positive change, with a leader's personality influencing organizational success. Authentic and conscious leadership, aligning needs and values, and self-leadership for adaptability are crucial.

The percentage of training is usually quite low in the business world, when compared to sports or the military. Deliberate practice, smart feedback, and a growth mindset that outperforms talent should be emphasized.

Cross-functional governance, collective intelligence, and dynamic teaming are pivotal for success in a fast-paced environment. A brilliant meta-leader empowers his team members and favored dynamic teaming by trust and freedom to operate with clear and simple rules.

The combination of psychological safety and task significance encourages and allows team members to be both separate wholes as well as act as part of something larger.

A successful teamwork implies win-win interactions where everyone benefits in some way and where the whole is greater than the sum of its parts.

Traditional top-down management approaches face limitations in the evolving complexity of challenges.

Only 20% of individuals and teams reach their full potential due to self-sabotage. Engaging in a mental fitness training plan will help you decrease your self-sabotage, and that of your team members.

Groups are remarkably intelligent under the right circumstances. A cross-functional governance meeting is key to build the culture of sharing needed to gain in speed, agility and hence effectiveness. By allowing people sharing and sometimes debating perspectives, it gave attendees the skills and confidence to better understand the global picture and solve their similar problems without the need for further guidance or clarification. At the end, it saved an incalculable amount of time that was no longer needed to seek clarification or permission.

Outsourcing is a way to expand its business without directly expanding its workforce. A key for success is to consider the partnerships as a team of teams.

The importance of regularly evaluating and measuring organizational health is stressed, using tools such as Positive Intelligence Quotient (PQ) and ISO 26000 standards.

If you enjoyed this book, please leave a positive review on Amazon. It would greatly help its distribution. Thank you in advance!

7 - REFERENCES

1. Antifragile: Things that Gain from Disorder., Nassim Nicholas Taleb, 2014

2. Atomic Habits: An Easy & Proven Way to Build Good Habits & Break Bad Ones, James Clear, 2018

3. Awaken the Giant Within: How to Take Immediate Control of Your Mental, Emotional, Physical & Financial Destiny, Anthony Robbins, 1991

4. Corporate Social Responsibility, https://www.belgium.be/en/economy/sustainable_development/sustainable_economy/corporate_social_responsibility

5. Corporate Social Responsibility (CSR) Explained With Examples, Jason Fernando, 2023, https://www.investopedia.com/terms/c/corp-social-responsibility.asp

6. Good to Great: Why Some Companies Make the Leap... and Others Don't, Jim Collins, 2004

7. Legacy: What the All Blacks Can Teach Us about the Business of Life, James Kerr, 2013

8. Mindset: The New Psychology of Success, Carol S. Dweck, 2007

9. Peak: How All of Us Can Achieve Extraordinary Things, Anders Ericsson & Robert Pool, 2017

10. Positive Intelligence: Why Only 20% Of Teams And Individuals Achieve Their True Potential And How You Can Achieve Yours, Shirzad Chamine, 2012

11. Success Factor Modeling Volume I, Next Generation Entrepreneurs: Live Your Dreams and Create a Better World Through Your Business, Robert B. Dilts, 2015

12. Success Factor Modeling Volume II, Generative Collaboration, Robert B. Dilts, 2016

13. Success Factor Modeling Volume III, Conscious Leadership and Resilience, Robert B. Dilts, 2017

14. Team of Teams, General Stanley McChrystal, 2015

15. The New One Minute Manager, Ken Blanchard & Spencer Johnson, 2015

16. The One Thing, Gary Keller & Jay Papasan, 2013

17. The Power of Mindset Change: Why Mindset Matters Most, Robert B Dilts & Mickey Feher, 2023

18. The Wisdom of Crowds, James Surowiecki , 2005

19. What Google Learned From Its Quest to Build the Perfect Team, Charles Duhigg, 2016, https://www.nytimes.com/2016/02/28/magazine/what-google-learned-from-its-quest-to-build-the-perfect-team.html

20. When The Impossible Becomes Possible - The Path to Self-Mastery and Letting Go, Laurent Zecchinon, 2023

21. Why We Do What We Do, Tony Robbins, 2006, TED talk, https://www.ted.com/talks/tony_robbins_why_we_do_what_we_do

22. Your Supply Chain Needs a Sustainability Strategy, Boston Consulting Group, 2020, https://www.bcg.com/publications/2020/supply-chain-needs-sustainability-strategy

ABOUT THE AUTHOR

I like to say that I lived two parallel lives until 2017, when I started to combine the two.

After a bachelor's degree in biochemistry followed by a doctorate, I worked for about twenty years in various Research & Development environments (university, SMEs, a multinational company, a secondary school & a hospital reference center).

A life at 200 miles per hour where I notably learned team and project management as well as strategic outsourcing (with all that implies in terms of governance, performance management, risks and issues management, quality, legal aspects, and procurement). I also experienced toxic management, biased evaluations, and abusive layoffs. All of this gave me a deep desire to learn how to manage differently and become a recognized agent of change in the field.

Karate (of which I am currently a 4th-degree black belt) and functional training (mainly at home) allowed me to stay on course during the more difficult times. I also had the opportunity to practice aikido, qi gong, yoga, and CrossFit. Over the years, I have observed individual and collective performance issues and have trained in communication in the broadest sense. It was a real revelation, and I realized that it was what truly motivated me.

In 2017, at the age of 44, a trip to the south of France and a CrossFit training inspired me to take action and train with the world's best. I then followed and obtained several coaching certifications in different areas to better understand and thus express all my potential.

I also discovered Biohacking, of which I have become a big fan, and which, in a way, connects my two lives. By combining ancestral knowledge (especially martial arts) and the most advanced scientific disciplines, it allows us to function optimally by providing many solutions to our modern daily constraints.

In 2021, I experienced difficult moments both personally and professionally. I then deepened the notions of resilience and antifragility, respectively through the work of **Boris Cyrulnik** and **Nassim Nicholas Taleb**. Today, richer, and stronger from all these experiences, I support individuals and organizations who want to regain control and improve their results in both their personal and professional lives.

Laurent Zecchinon

Website

https://laurentzecchinon.com

Facebook Page (in French)

https://www.facebook.com/lzecchinon.coaching.biohacking

YouTube Channel (in French)

Laurent Zecchinon - Coaching & Biohacking
https://www.youtube.com/channel/UCFZc-
S7wxQgUMG_EufSIz6w

Linkedin Profile

https://www.linkedin.com/in/laurent-zecchinon/